Easy Piano

My First Song Book
Volume 2

A TREASURY OF FAVORITE SONGS TO SING AND PLAY

ISBN 978-0-634-04792-3

Walt Disney Music Company
Wonderland Music Company, Inc.

DISTRIBUTED BY

Visit Hal Leonard Online at
www.halleonard.com

Contact us:
Hal Leonard
7777 West Bluemound Road
Milwaukee, WI 53213
Email: info@halleonard.com

In Europe, contact:
Hal Leonard Europe Limited
42 Wigmore Street
Marylebone, London, W1U 2RN
Email: info@halleonardeurope.com

In Australia, contact:
Hal Leonard Australia Pty. Ltd.
4 Lentara Court
Cheltenham, Victoria, 3192 Australia
Email: info@halleonard.com.au

Contents

My Funny Friend and Me

from Walt Disney Pictures' *The Emperor's New Groove*

Lyrics by Sting • Music by Sting and David Hartley

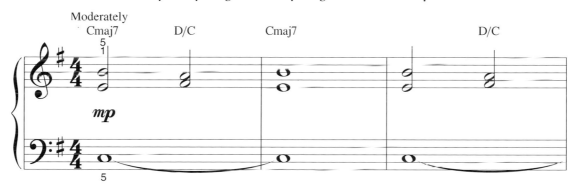

In the qui - et time of eve - ning,
that the world is not my play - ground;

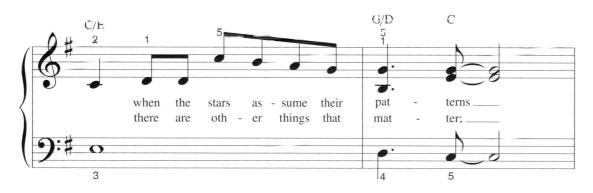

when the stars as - sume their pat - terns _____
there are oth - er things that mat - ter;

and the day has made his jour - ney,
what is sim - ple needs pro - tect - ing.

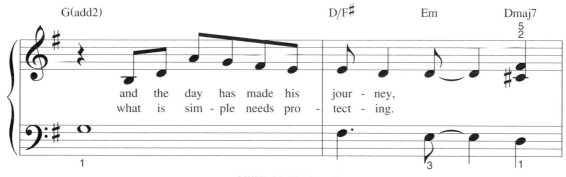

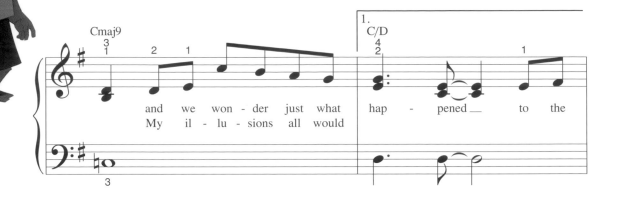

and we won - der just what / hap - pened ____ to the
My il - lu - sions all would

life we knew, ____ be - fore the world changed, ____ when not a

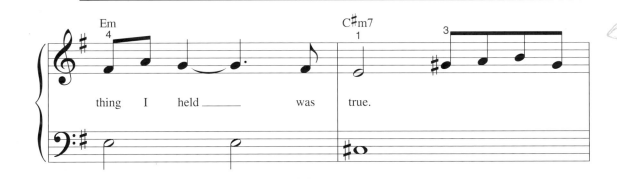

thing I held _____ was true.

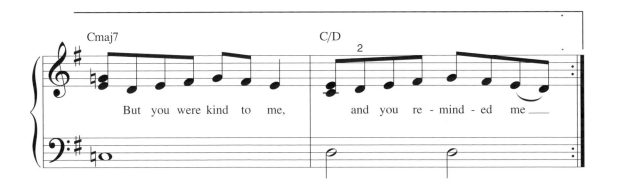

But you were kind to me, / and you re - mind - ed me ____

shat - ter, _____ but you stayed _____ in my

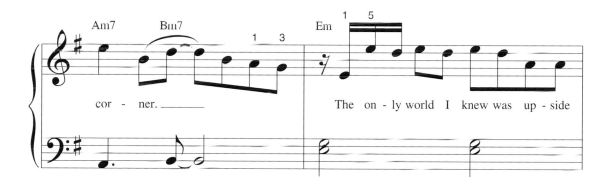

cor - ner. _____ The on - ly world I knew was up - side

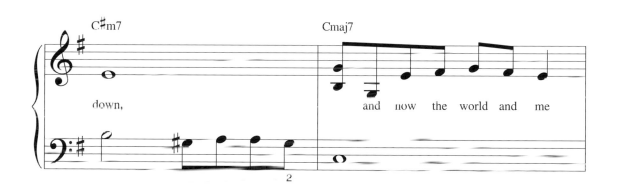

down, and now the world and me

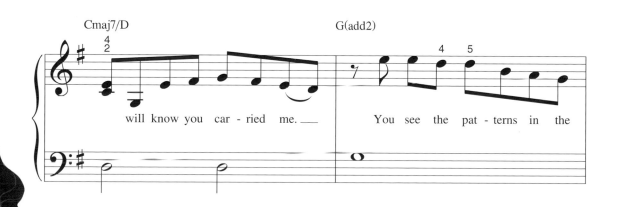

will know you car - ried me. _____ You see the pat - terns in the

D/F#   Em7   D   Cmaj7

big   sky; ___   those con - stel - la - tions look like

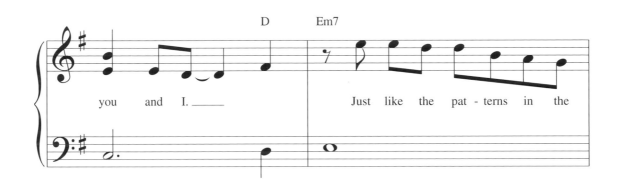

D   Em7

you   and   I. ___   Just like the pat - terns in the

Bm7   C#m7♭5

big   sky, ___   we could be lost; we could re -

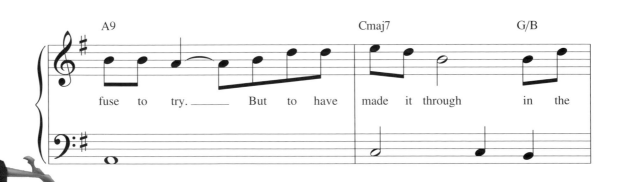

A9   Cmaj7   G/B

fuse to   try. ___ But to have   made it through   in the

dark night,

who would those luck - y guys turn out to

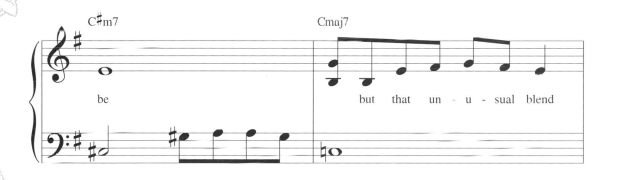

be

but that un - u - sual blend

of my fun - ny friend and me.

I'm not as clev - er as I

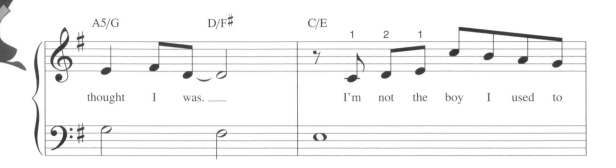

A5/G   D/F#   C/E

thought I was. ___ I'm not the boy I used to

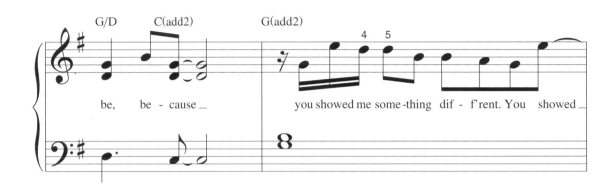

G/D C(add2) G(add2)

be, be - cause ___ you showed me some-thing dif - f'rent. You showed ___

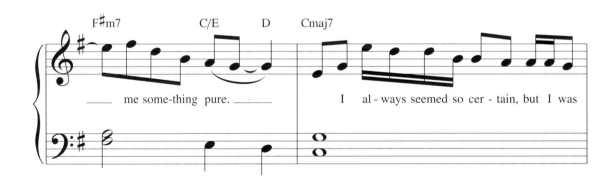

F#m7 C/E D Cmaj7

___ me some-thing pure. ___ I al - ways seemed so cer - tain, but I was

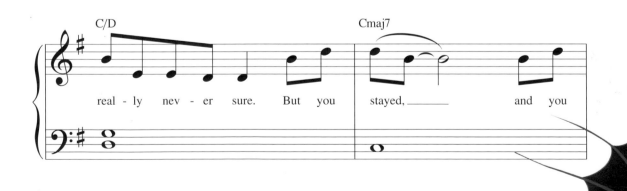

C/D   Cmaj7

real - ly nev - er sure. But you stayed, ___ and you

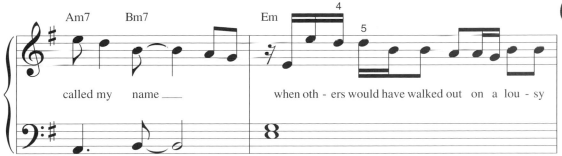

called my   name _____   when oth - ers would have walked out   on a lou - sy

game.   And look who made it through   but your fun - ny friend and

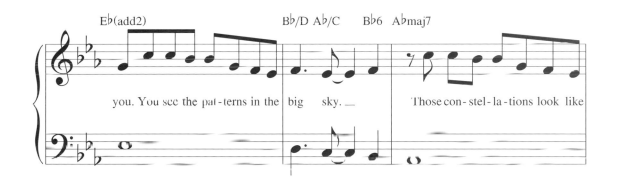

you. You see the pat - terns in the big   sky. _____   Those con - stel - la - tions look like

you   and I. _____   That ti - ny plan - et and the   big - ger guy. _____

Abmaj7 ... Bb7sus

I don't know wheth-er I should laugh or cry.

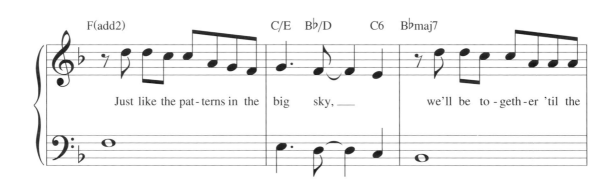

F(add2) ... C/E Bb/D C6 Bbmaj7

Just like the pat-terns in the big sky, ___ we'll be to-geth-er 'til the

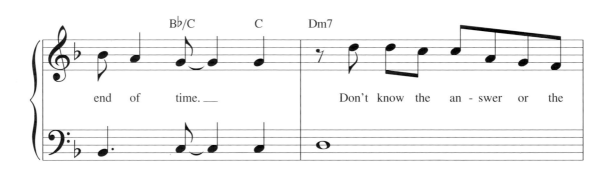

Bb/C C Dm7

end of time. ___ Don't know the an-swer or the

Dm/C Bm7b5 G9

rea-son why. ___ We'll stick to-geth-er 'til the day we die. ___

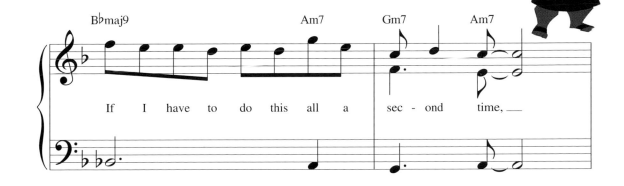

If I have to do this all a sec-ond time, __

I won't com-plain or make a fuss. Who would the an-gels send,

but that un-like-ly blend of these two fun-ny friends? That's us. __

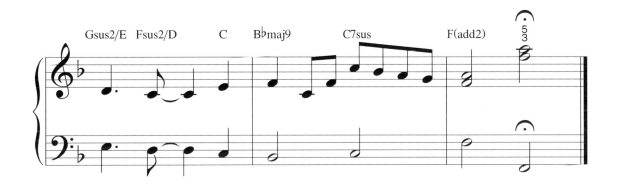

SOMEDAY

from Walt Disney's *The Hunchback of Notre Dame*

Music by Alan Menken • Lyrics by Stephen Schwartz

Some - day when we are

wis - er, when the world's old - er, when we have

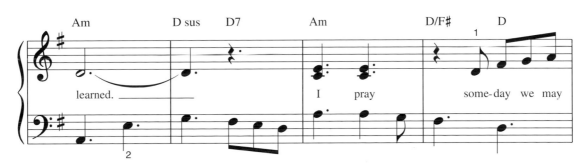

learned. _____ I pray some-day we may

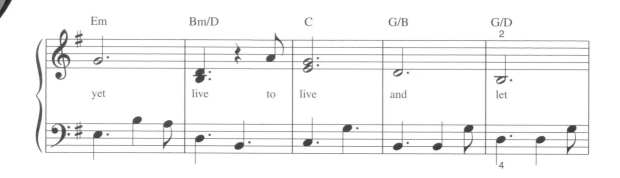

yet   live   to   live   and   let

live.   Some - day   life will be fair - er,

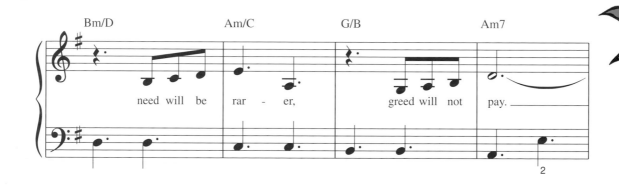

need will be rar - er,   greed will not pay. ___

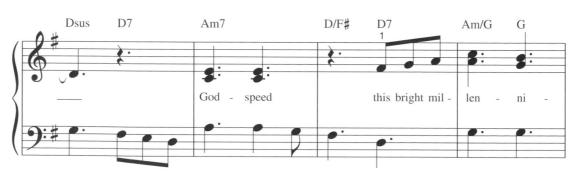

___   God - speed   this bright mil - len - ni -

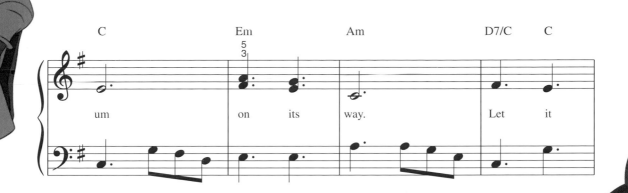

um   on   its   way.   Let   it

come   some - day.

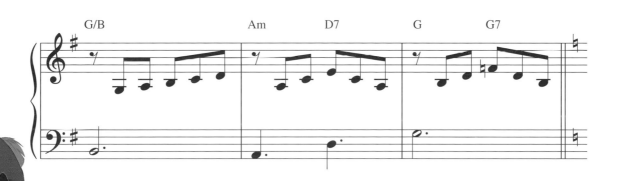

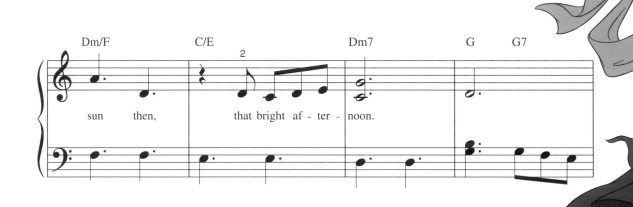

C   **Em/B**   **F/A**   **Em/G**

Some - day   our fight will be   won   then,   we'll stand in the

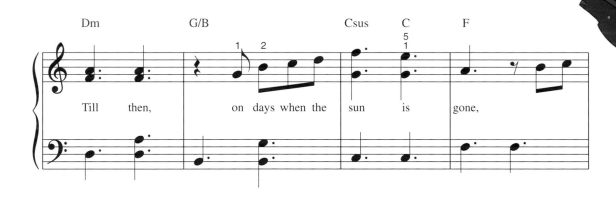

Dm/F   **C/E**   **Dm7**   **G**   **G7**

sun   then,   that bright af - ter - noon.

Dm   **G/B**   **Csus**   **C**   **F**

Till   then,   on days when the   sun   is   gone,

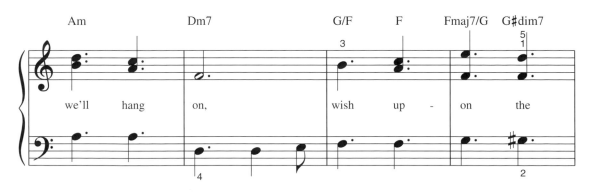

Am   **Dm7**   **G/F**   **F**   **Fmaj7/G**   **G#dim7**

we'll   hang   on,   wish   up - on   the

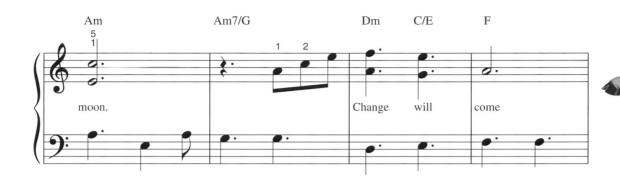

moon.   Change   will   come

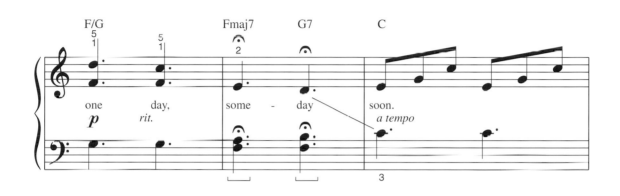

one   day,   some - day   soon.

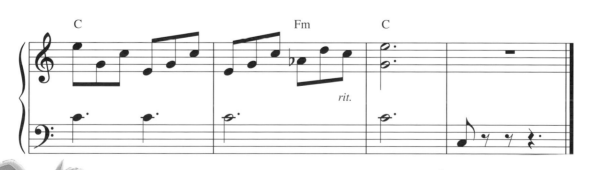

God Help the Outcasts

from Walt Disney's *The Hunchback of Notre Dame*

Music by Alan Menken • Lyrics by Stephen Schwartz

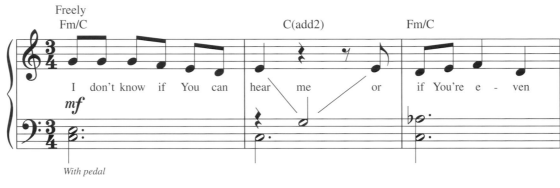

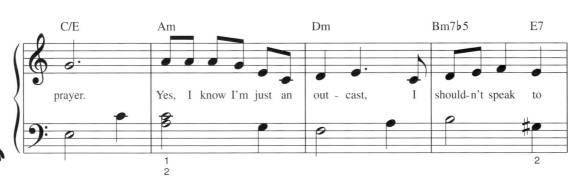

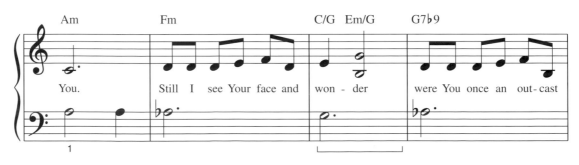

Moderately

too?

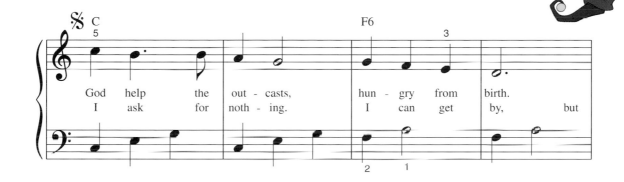

God help the out - casts, hun - gry from birth.
I ask for noth - ing. I can get by, but

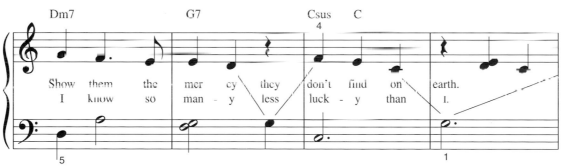

Show them the mer - cy they don't find on earth.
I know so man - y less luck - y than I.

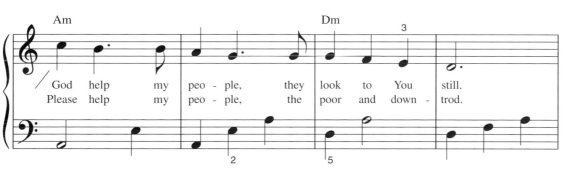

God help my peo - ple, they look to You still.
Please help my peo - ple, the poor and down - trod.

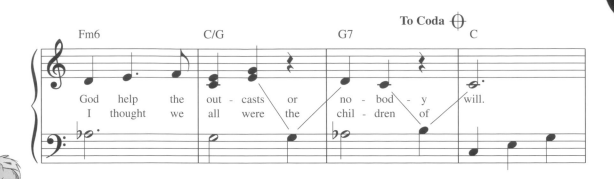

God help the out - casts or no - bod - y will.
I thought we all were the chil - dren of

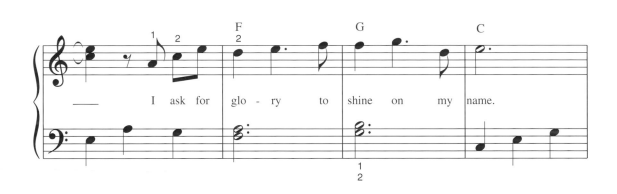

I ask for wealth. I ask for fame.

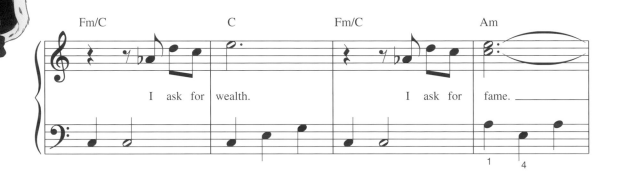

I ask for glo - ry to shine on my name.

I ask for love I can pos - sess.

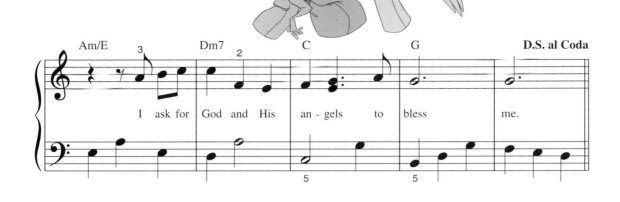

I ask for God and His an-gels to bless me.

CODA

Slower

God. _____ God help the out-casts

chil-dren of God.

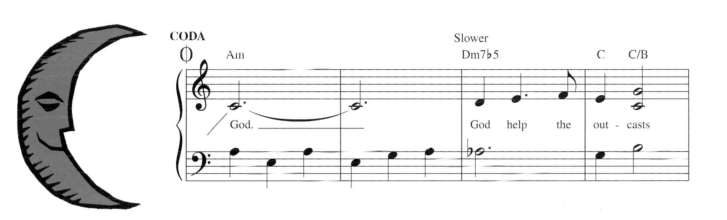

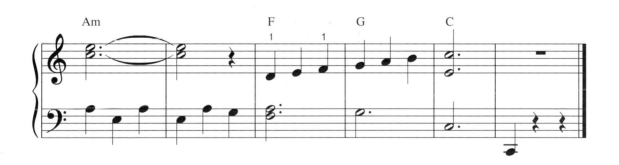

It's a Small World

from Disneyland and Walt Disney World's

It's a Small World

Words and Music by Richard M. Sherman and Robert B. Sherman

Brisk March tempo

It's a world of laugh - ter, a
There is a world just one moon and one

world of tears, it's a world of
gold - en sun, and a smile means

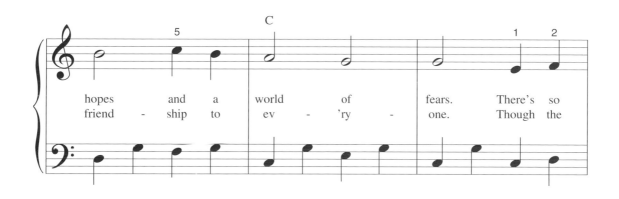

hopes and a world of fears. There's so
friend - ship to ev - 'ry - one. Though the

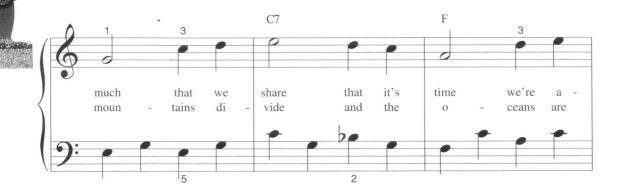

much   that   we   share   that   it's   time   we're   a -
moun - tains di - vide   and   the   o - ceans   are

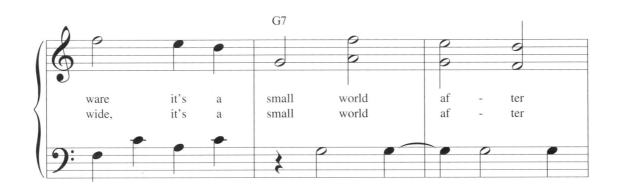

ware   it's   a   small   world   af - ter
wide,   it's   a   small   world   af - ter

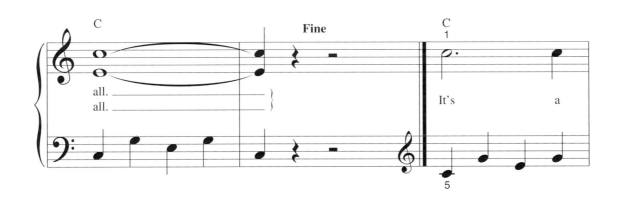

Fine

all.
all.   It's   a

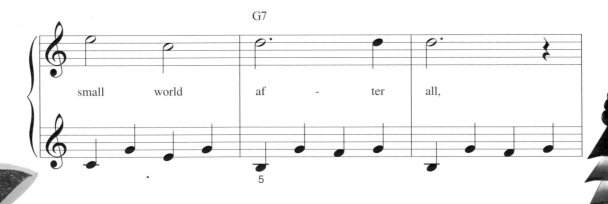

small   world   af - ter   all,

it's a small world af - ter

all, it's a small world

af - ter all, it's a small,

small world.

D.C. al Fine

Can You Feel the Love Tonight

from Walt Disney Pictures' *The Lion King*

Music by Elton John • Lyrics by Tim Rice

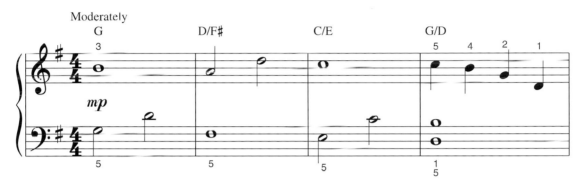

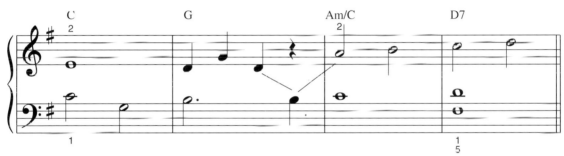

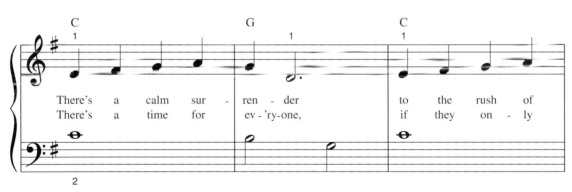

There's a calm sur - ren - der to the rush of
There's a time for ev - 'ry-one, if they on - ly

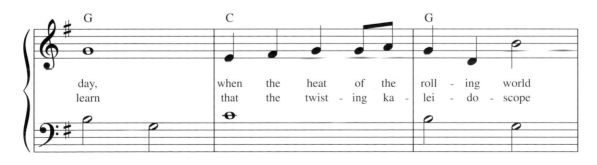

day, when the heat of the roll - ing world
learn that the twist - ing ka - lei - do - scope

can be turned a - way.
moves us all in turn.

An en - chant - ed
There's a rhyme and

mo - ment,
rea - son

and it sees me through.
to the wild out - doors

It's e - nough for this
when the heart of this

rest - less war - rior
star - crossed voy - ag - er

just to be with
beats in time with

you.
yours.

And can you feel the love

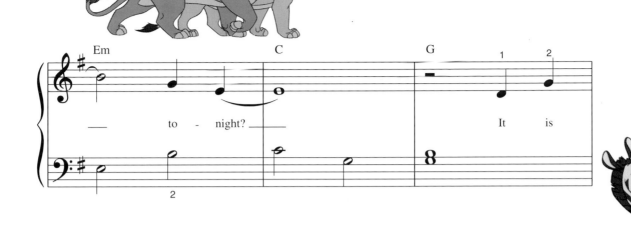

to - night? It is

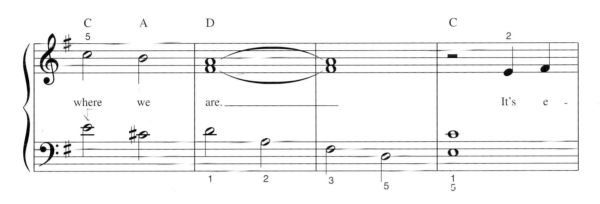

where we are. It's e -

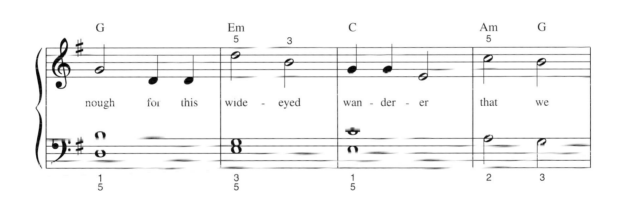

nough for this wide - eyed wan - der - er that we

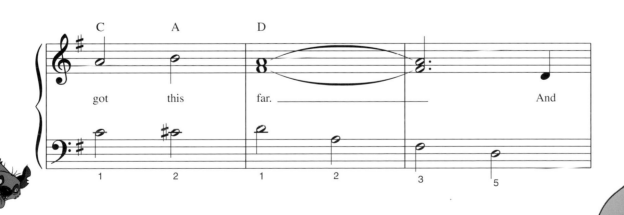

got this far. And

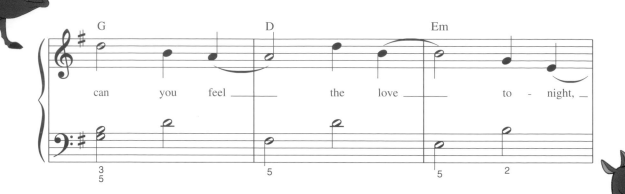

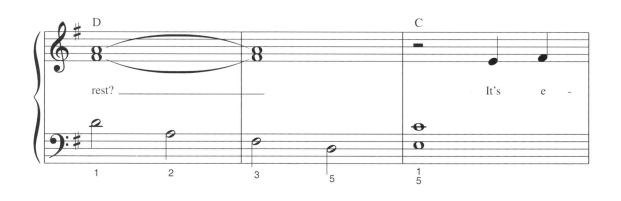

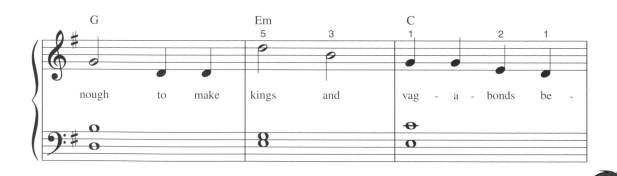

Kiss the Girl

from Walt Disney's *The Little Mermaid*

Lyrics by Howard Ashman • Music by Alan Menken

Lyrics (as they appear under the staff):

There you see her sit-ting there a-cross the way. She don't got a lot to say, but there's some-thing a-bout her. And you

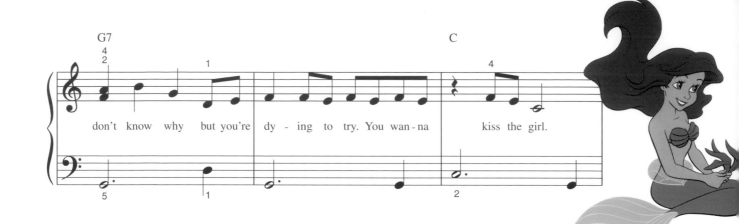

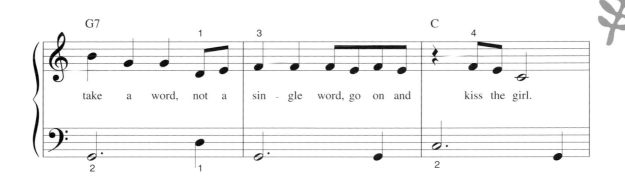

take   a   word,   not   a   sin - gle   word, go   on   and   kiss   the   girl.

Sha   la   la   la   la   la   my   oh   my. Look like the

boy   too   shy. Ain't gon - na   kiss   the   girl.   Sha   la   la   la   la   la

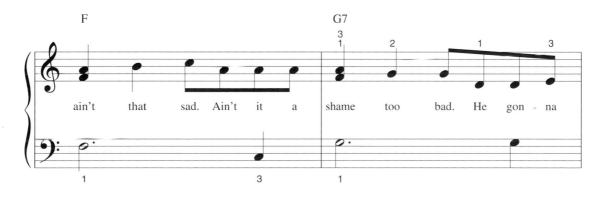

ain't   that   sad. Ain't   it   a   shame   too   bad. He gon - na

miss the girl.

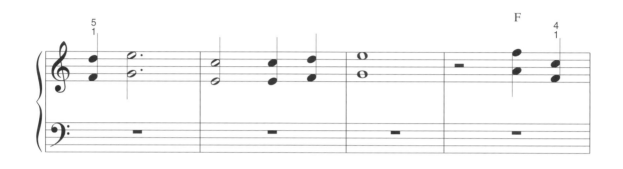

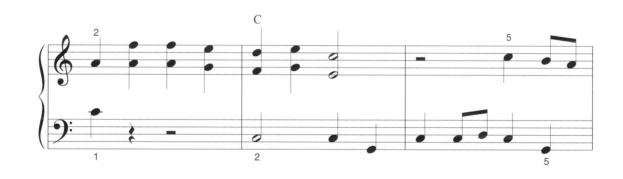

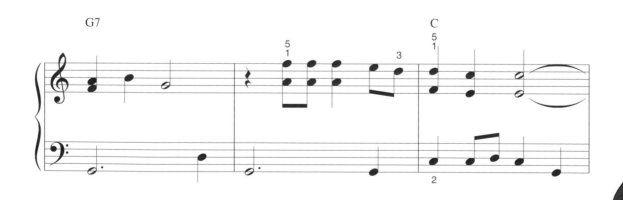

Now's   your   mo - ment,   float-ing in a blue la -

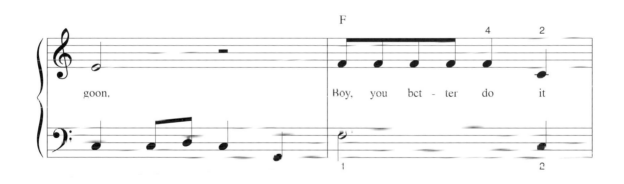

goon,   Boy, you bet - ter do   it

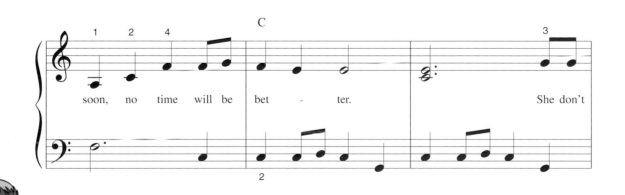

soon, no time will be   bet -   ter.   She don't

say a word and she won't say a word un - til you

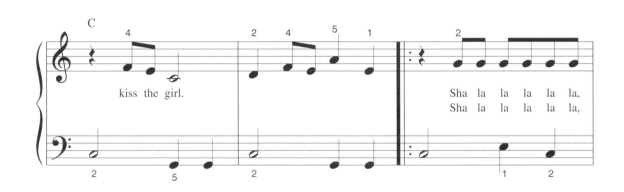

kiss the girl.

Sha la la la la la,
Sha la la la la la,

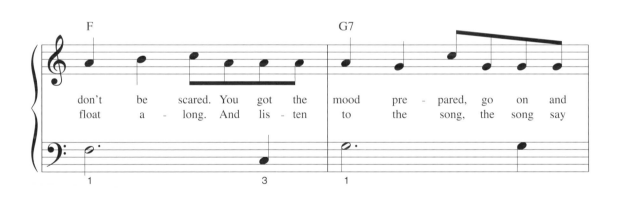

don't be scared. You got the mood pre - pared, go on and
float a - long. And lis - ten to the song, the song say

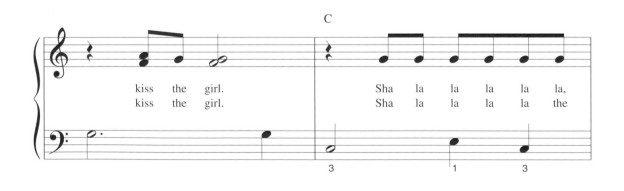

kiss the girl.
kiss the girl.

Sha la la la la la,
Sha la la la la the

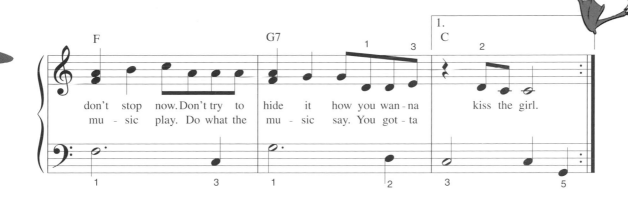

don't stop now. Don't try to | hide it how you wan - na | kiss the girl.
mu - sic play. Do what the | mu - sic say. You got - ta |

kiss the girl. | You've got to | kiss the girl.

You wan - na | kiss the girl. | You've got - ta | kiss the girl.

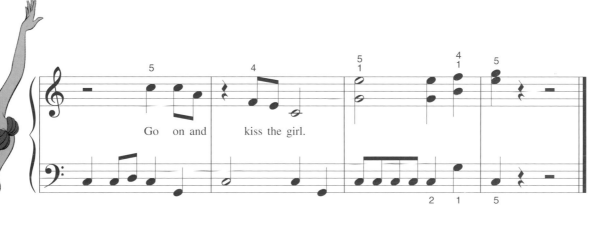

Go on and | kiss the girl.

Part of Your World

from Walt Disney's *The Little Mermaid*

Lyrics by Howard Ashman • Music by Alan Menken

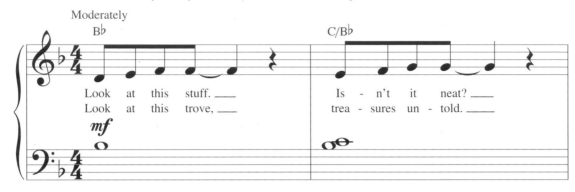

Moderately

B♭ — Look at this stuff. ___ / Look at this trove, ___
C/B♭ — Is -n't it neat? ___ / trea - sures un - told. ___

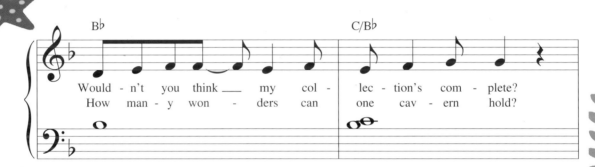

B♭ — Would -n't you think ___ my col - / How man - y won - ders can
C/B♭ — lec - tion's com - plete? / one cav - ern hold?

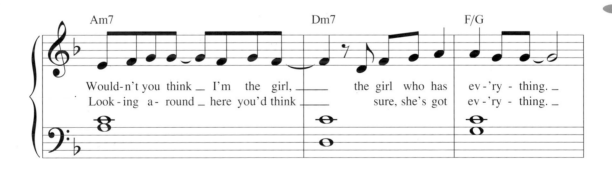

Am7 — Would-n't you think __ I'm the girl, ___ / Look-ing a - round __ here you'd think ___
Dm7 — the girl who has / sure, she's got
F/G — ev - 'ry - thing. __ / ev - 'ry - thing. __

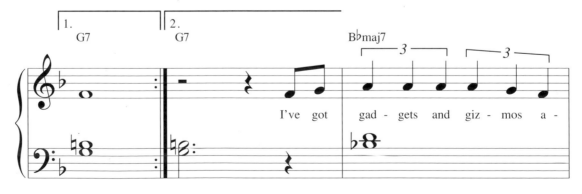

1. **G7**   **2.** **G7**

B♭maj7 — I've got gad - gets and giz - mos a -

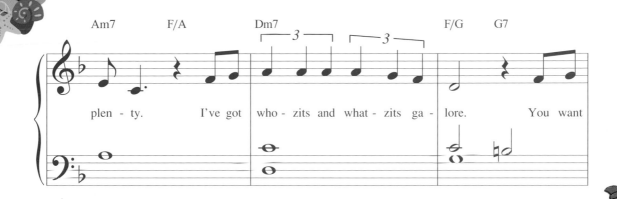

plen - ty.   I've got   who - zits and what - zits ga - lore.   You want

thing - a - ma - bobs,   I've got   twen - ty.   But who   cares?   No big

deal.   I   want   more,

I wan - na be ___ where the   peo - ple are.   I wan - na see ___ wan - na
Flip - pin' your fins ___ you don't   get too far.   Legs are re - quired ___ for

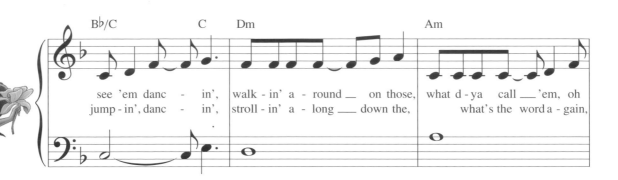

see 'em danc - in', walk - in' a - round ___ on those, what d - ya call ___ 'em, oh
jump - in', danc - in', stroll - in' a - long ___ down the, what's the word a - gain,

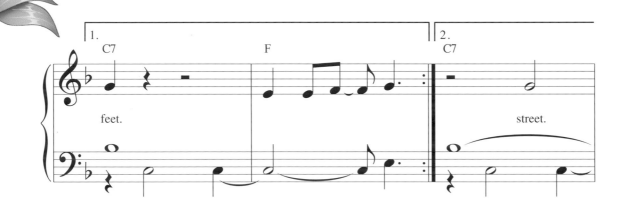

feet. street.

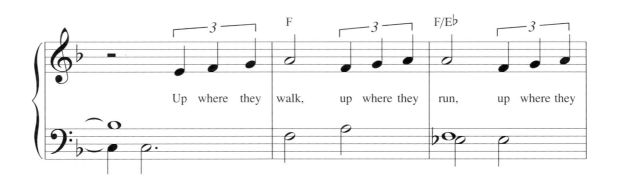

Up where they walk, up where they run, up where they

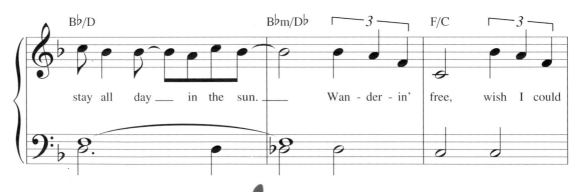

stay all day ___ in the sun. ___ Wan - der - in' free, wish I could

be   part   of that   world. _____   What would   I

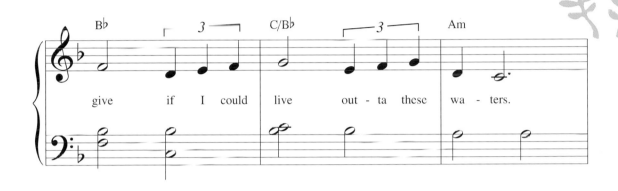

give   if I could   live   out - ta these   wa - ters.

What would I   pay   to spend a   day   warm on the

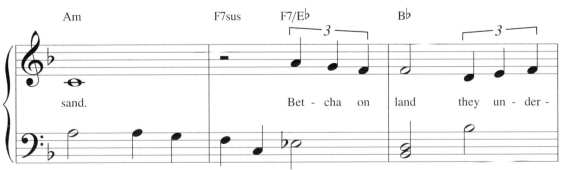

sand.   Bet - cha on   land   they un - der -

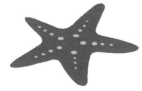

C/B♭   A7sus   A7   Dm   Dm/C

stand.   Bet they don't   re - pri - mand ___ their daugh - ters.   Bright young

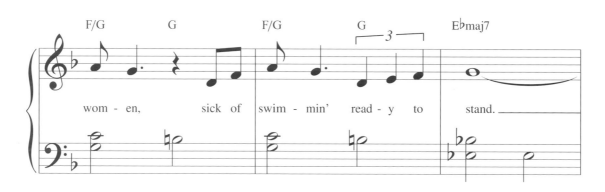

F/G   G   F/G   G   E♭maj7

wom - en,   sick of   swim - min'   read - y   to   stand. ___

B♭/C   F   Am7

___   And   read - y   to   know ___ what the   peo - ple   know. ___

B♭   C7   Dm

Ask 'em my ques - tions and   get some an - swers.   What's a fire, ___ and

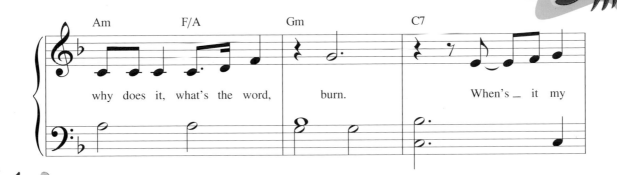

why does it, what's the word, burn.

When's __ it my

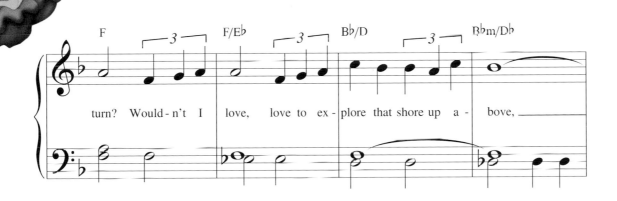

turn? Would-n't I love, love to ex-plore that shore up a-bove, _____

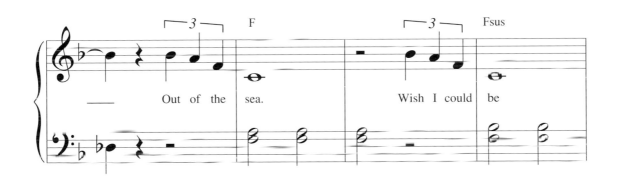

_____ Out of the sea. Wish I could be

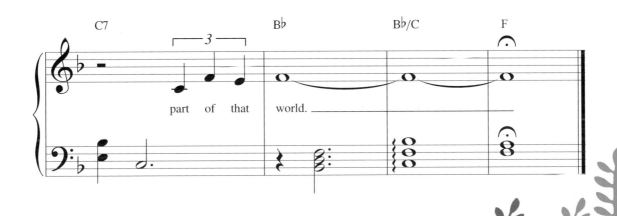

part of that world. _____

Chim Chim Cher-ee

from Walt Disney's *Mary Poppins*

Words and Music by Richard M. Sherman and Robert B. Sherman

Lightly, with gusto

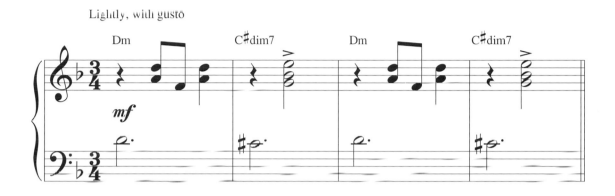

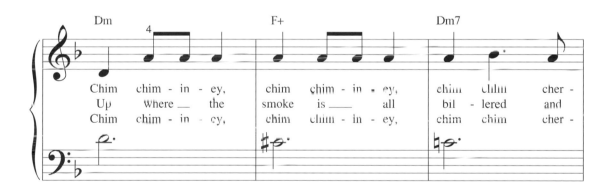

Chim chim - in - ey, chim chim - in - ey, chim chim cher -
Up where __ the smoke is __ all bil - lered and
Chim chim - in - ey, chim chim - in - ey, chim chim cher -

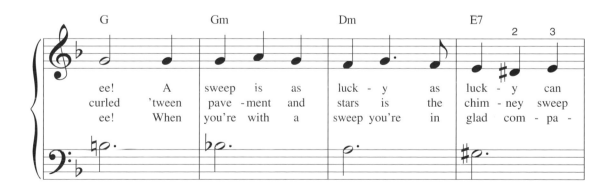

ee! A sweep is as luck - y as luck - y can
curled 'tween pave - ment and stars is the chim - ney sweep
ee! When you're with a sweep you're in glad com - pa -

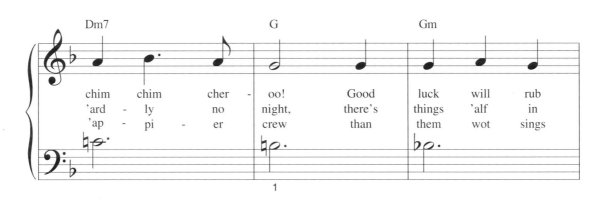

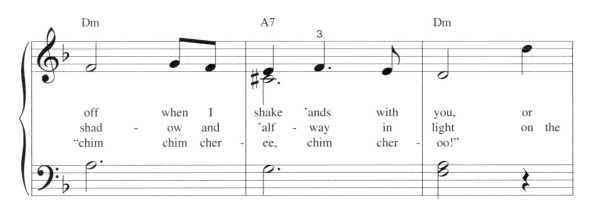

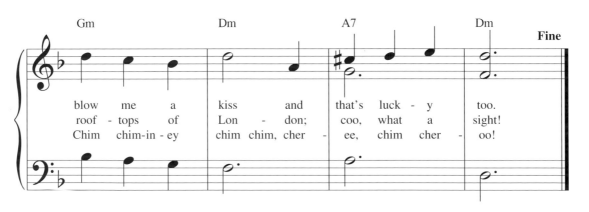

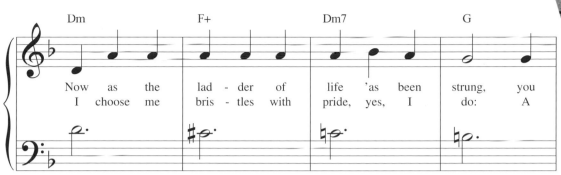

Dm | **F+** | **Dm7** | **G**

Now as the | lad - der of | life 'as been | strung, you
I choose me | bris - tles with | pride, yes, I | do: A

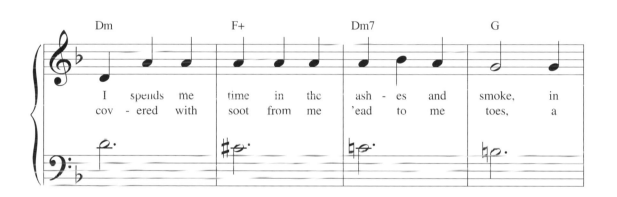

Gm | **Dm** | **E7** | **A**

may think a | sweep's on the | bot - tom - most | rung. Though
broom for the | shaft and a | brush for the | flue. Though I'm

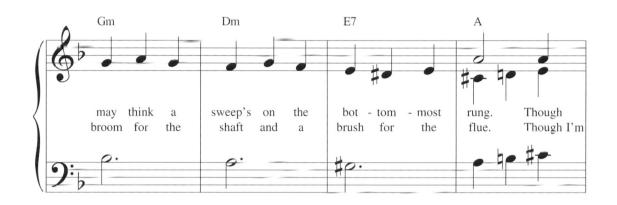

Dm | **F+** | **Dm7** | **G**

I spends me | time in the | ash - es and | smoke, in
cov - ered with | soot from me | 'ead to me | toes, a

Gm | **Dm** | **A7** | **Dm** (D.C.)

this 'ole wide | world there's no | 'ap - pi - er | bloke.
sweep knows 'e's | wel - come wher - | ev - er 'e | goes.

51

Supercalifragilisticexpialidocious

from Walt Disney's *Mary Poppins*

Words and Music by Richard M. Sherman and Robert B. Sherman

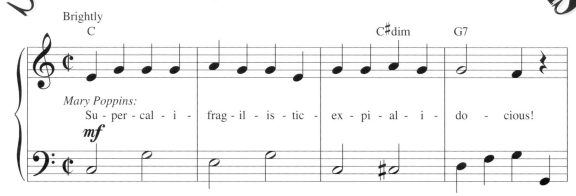

Brightly

Mary Poppins:
Su - per - cal - i - frag - il - is - tic - ex - pi - al - i - do - cious!

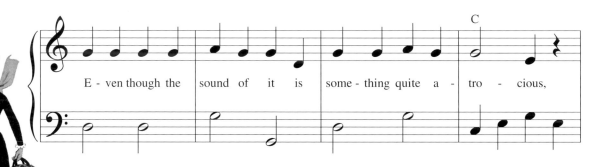

E - ven though the sound of it is some - thing quite a - tro - cious,

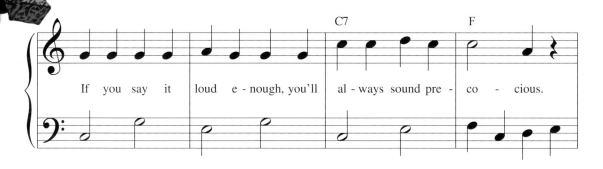

If you say it loud e - nough, you'll al - ways sound pre - co - cious.

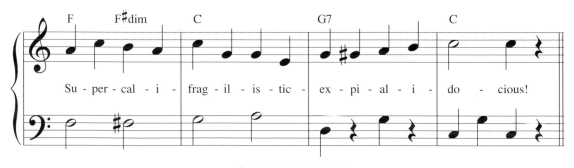

Su - per - cal - i - frag - il - is - tic - ex - pi - al - i - do - cious!

Pearlies: Um did-dle did-dle did-dle, um did-dle ay! Um did-dle did-dle did-dle,

um did-dle ay!

Bert: Be-
Mary{ He
Poppins:{ So

cause I was a-fraid to speak when
trav-elled all a-round the world and
when the cat has got your tongue, there's

I was just a lad,
ev-'ry-where he went,
no need to dis-may.

me fa-ther gave me
he'd use his word and
Just sum-mon up this

nose a tweak and
all would say, "There
word and then you've

told me I was
goes a clev-er
got a lot to

bad.
gent!"
say.

But then one day I
Bert:{ When dukes and ma-'a-
{ But bet-ter use it

Reflection

from Walt Disney Pictures' *Mulan*

Music by Matthew Wilder • Lyrics by David Zippel

Mulan: Look at me, I will nev-er pass for a per-fect bride or a per-fect daugh-ter. Can it be I'm not meant to play this part? Now I see that if

Am7 — Dm7 — Dm7♭5

I were tru - ly to be my-self, I would break my fam - 'ly's ___

C — Am7

heart. ___ Who is that girl I ___ see

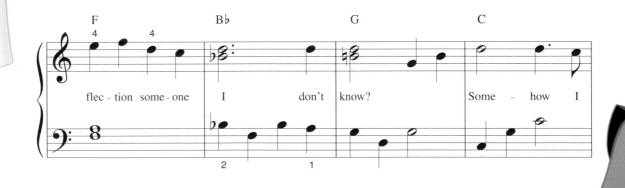

G/F — F — Fm — C — G/B — Am

star - ing straight back at me? Why is my re -

F — B♭ — G — C

flec - tion some - one I don't know? Some - how I

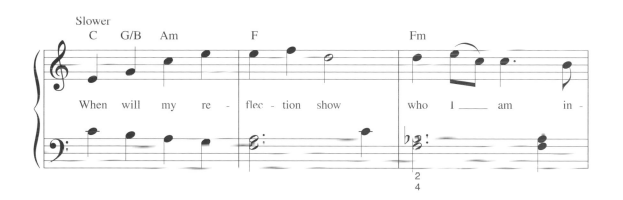

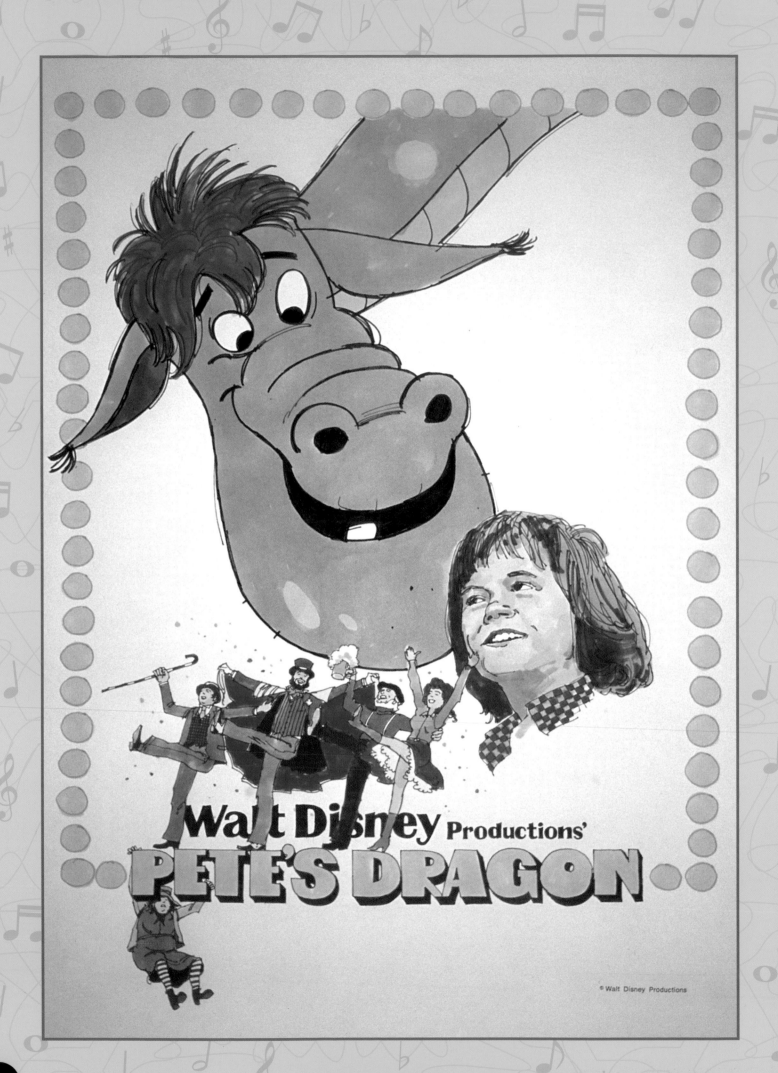

Candle on the Water

from Walt Disney's *Pete's Dragon*

Words and Music by Al Kasha and Joel Hirschhorn

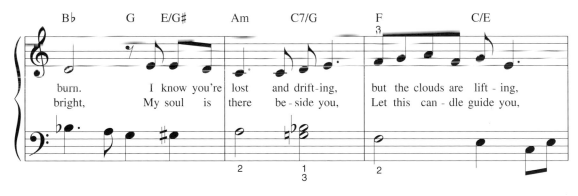

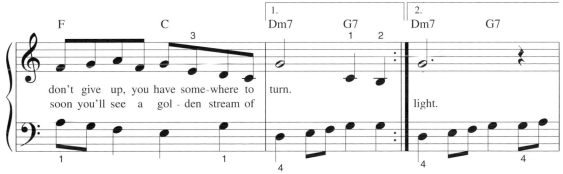

B♭   C7   F   B♭   C7

A cold and friend-less tide has found you,   Don't let the storm-y dark-ness

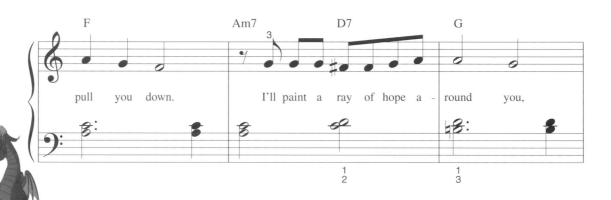

F   Am7   D7   G

pull you down.   I'll paint a ray of hope a - round you,

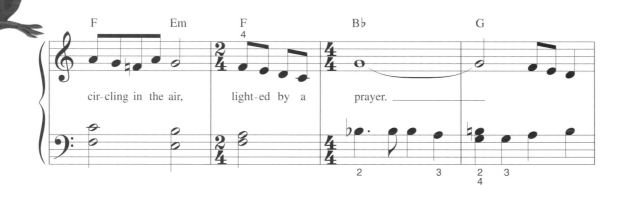

F   Em   F   B♭   G

cir-cling in the air,   light-ed by a   prayer.

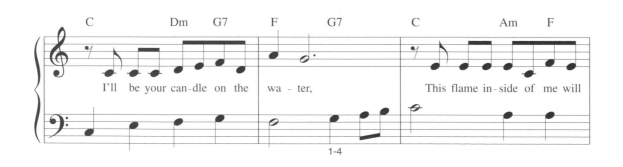

C   Dm   G7   F   G7   C   Am   F

I'll be your can-dle on the   wa - ter,   This flame in-side of me will

1-4

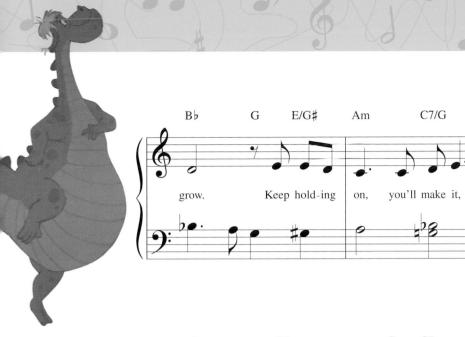

Bb   G   E/G#   Am   C7/G   F   C/E

grow.   Keep hold-ing on, you'll make it, Here's my hand, so take it,

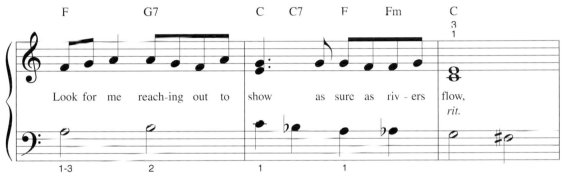

F   G7   C C7 F Fm C

Look for me reach-ing out to show as sure as riv - ers flow,
rit.

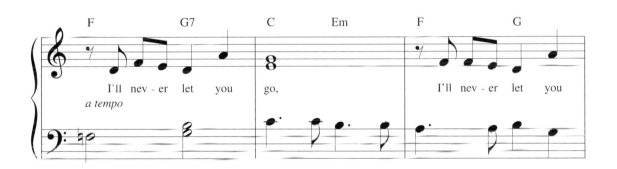

F   G7   C   Em   F   G

I'll nev - er let you go, I'll nev - er let you
a tempo

C Em F G7 C   F C

go, I'll nev-er let you go.

The Second Star to the Right

from Walt Disney's *Peter Pan*

Words Sammy Cahn • Music by Sammy Fain

Slowly, with expression

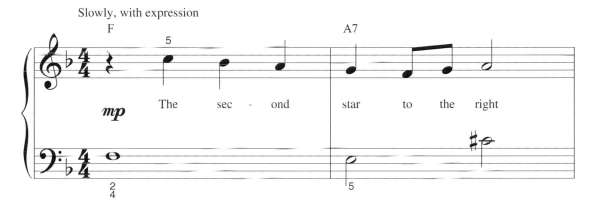

The sec - ond star to the right

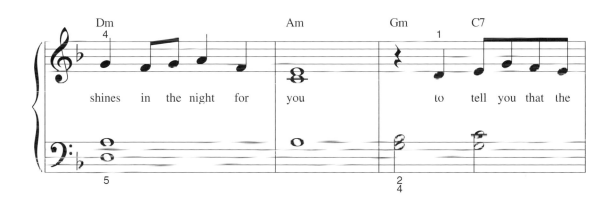

shines in the night for you to tell you that the

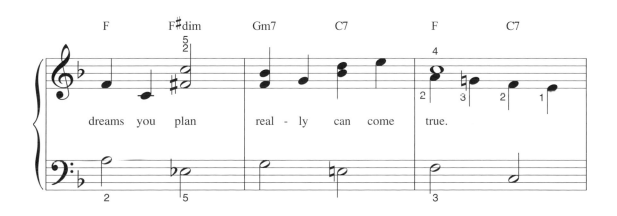

dreams you plan real - ly can come true.

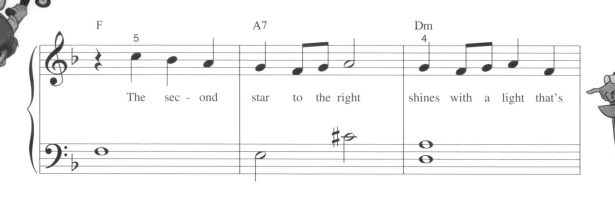

The sec - ond star to the right shines with a light that's

rare, and if it's Nev - er Land you need, its

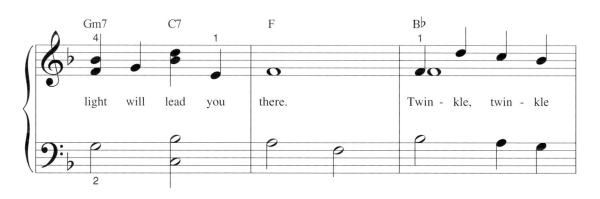

light will lead you there. Twin - kle, twin - kle

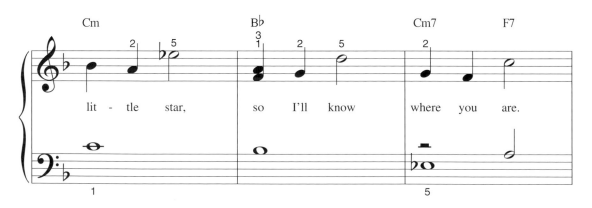

lit - tle star, so I'll know where you are.

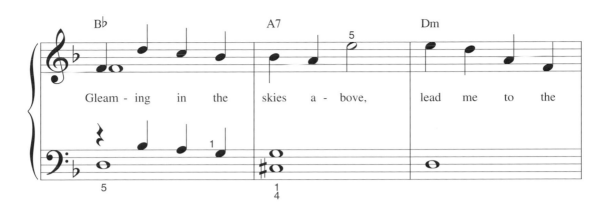

Gleam - ing in the skies a - bove, lead me to the

one who loves me. And when you bring him my way,

slower   *a tempo*

each time we say, "Good - night," we'll thank the lit - tle

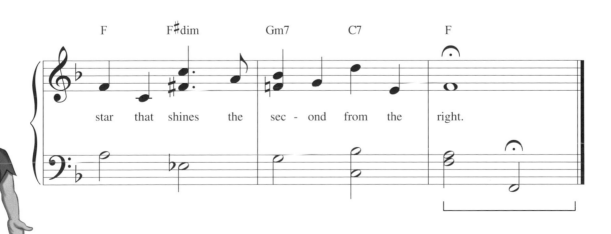

star that shines the sec - ond from the right.

You'll Be in My Heart
(Pop Version)

As Performed by Phil Collins

from Walt Disney Pictures' *Tarzan*™

Words and Music by Phil Collins

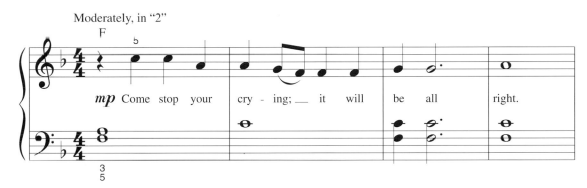

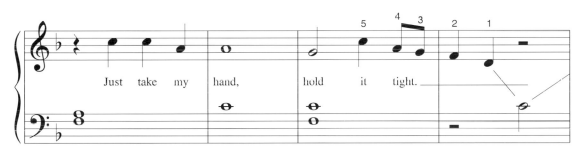

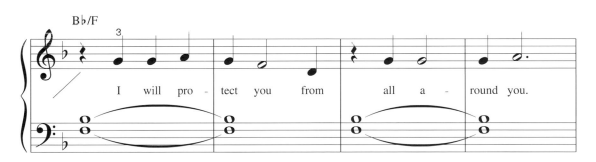

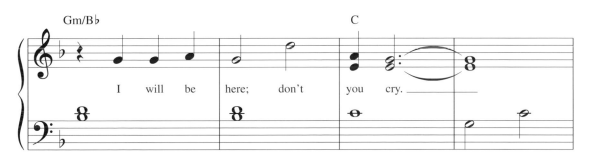

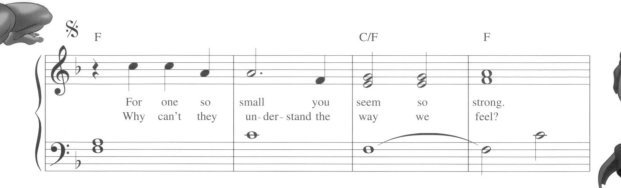

%
F   C/F   F

For   one   so   small   you   seem   so   strong.
Why   can't   they   un - der - stand the   way   we   feel?

                                                              C/F

My   arms   will   hold   you, __   keep   you   safe   and
They   just   don't   trust _____   what   they   can't   ex -

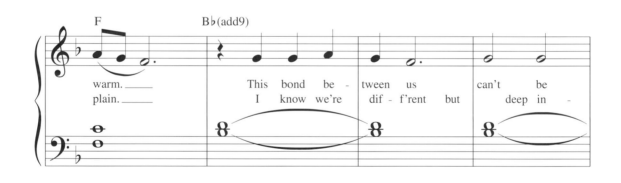

F   Bb(add9)

warm. _____   This   bond   be -   tween   us   can't   be
plain. _____   I   know   we're   dif - f'rent   but   deep   in -

                Gm   C

bro - ken.   I   will   be   here;   don't   you   cry. ___
side   us.   We're   not   that   dif - fer - ent   at   all. ___

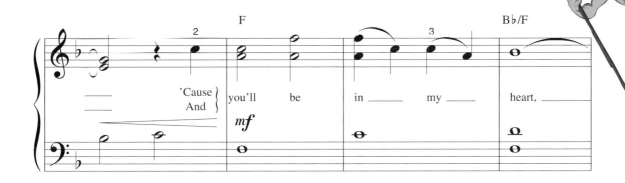

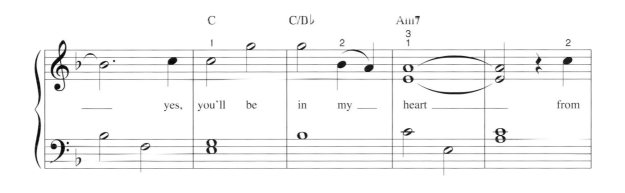

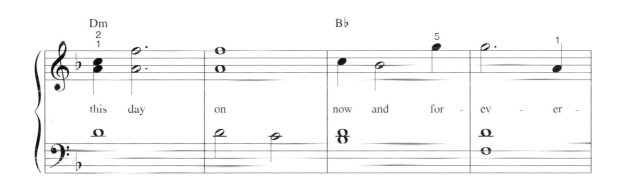

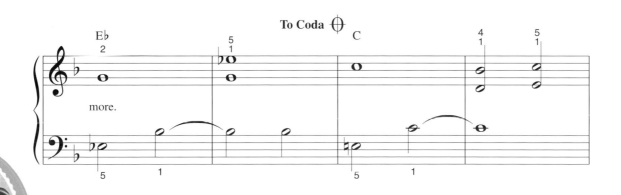

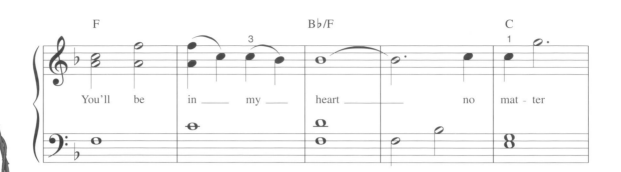

You'll be in my heart no mat - ter

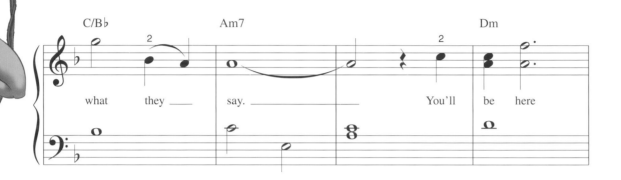

what they say. You'll be here

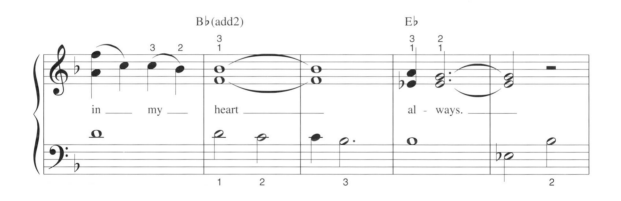

in my heart al - ways.

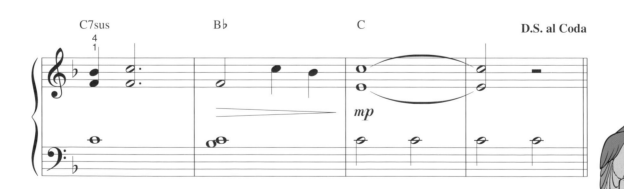

D.S. al Coda

mp

CODA

C   Fsus2

Don't   lis - ten   to   them,
mp   des - ti - ny   calls ____

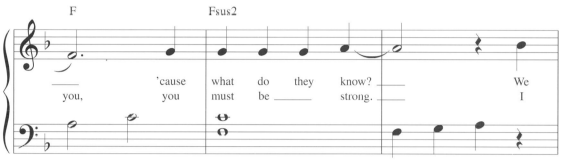

F   Fsus2

____   'cause   what   do   they   know? ____   We
you,   you   must   be ____ strong. ____   I

Fsus/D   F(add9)/C   Dm7

need   each   oth - er   to   have,   to   hold.
may   not   be   with   you,   but you've   got   to   hold   on.

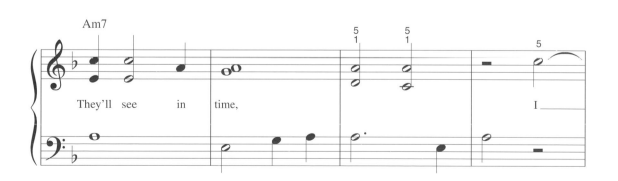

Am7

They'll   see   in   time,   I ____

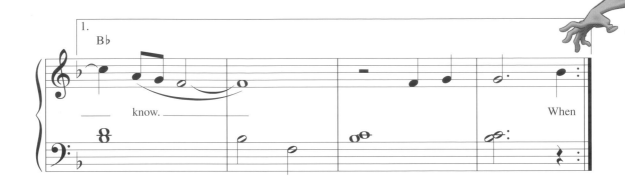

know.

When

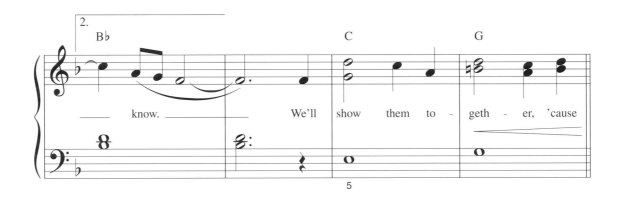

know.

We'll show them to - geth - er, 'cause

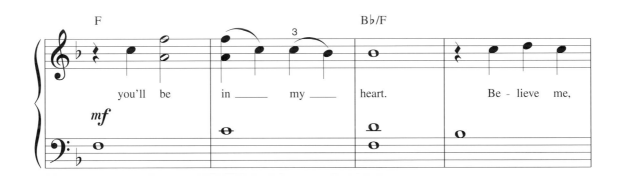

you'll be in my heart.

Be - lieve me,

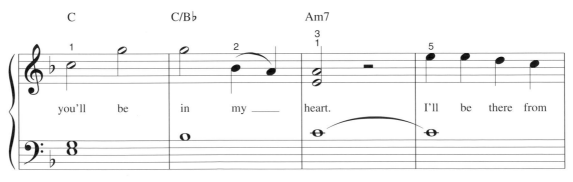

you'll be in my heart.

I'll be there from

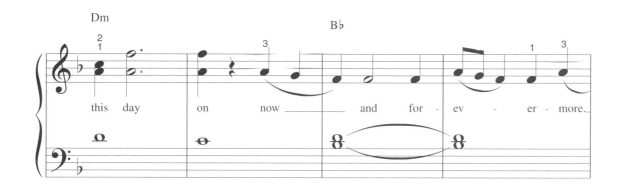

Dm — this day — on — now ____ and for - ev - er - more.

Bb

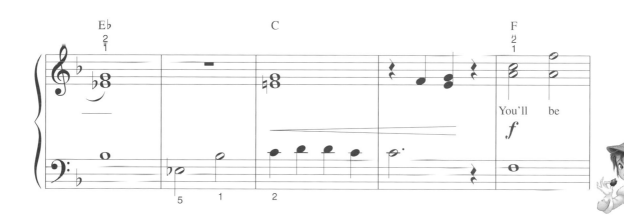

Eb — C — F — You'll be *f*

Bb/F — in ____ my ____ heart — (You'll be here in my heart.) — no mat - ter

C

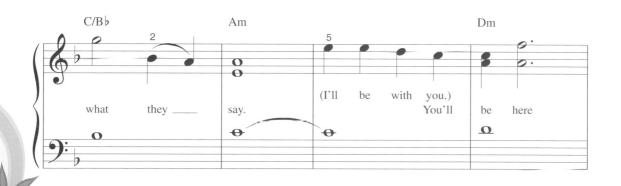

C/Bb — what they ____ say. — Am — (I'll be with you.) You'll be here — Dm

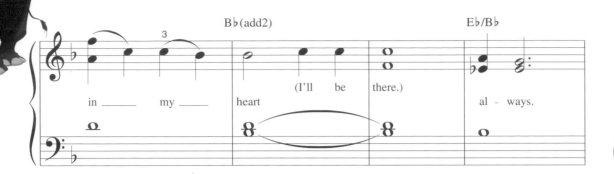

Bb(add2)　　　　　　　　　　　　　　Eb/Bb

in ___ my ___ heart　(I'll be there.)　al - ways.

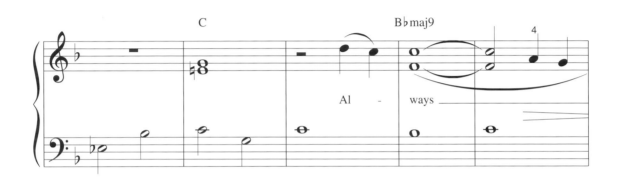

C　　　　　　　　　Bbmaj9

Al - ways ___

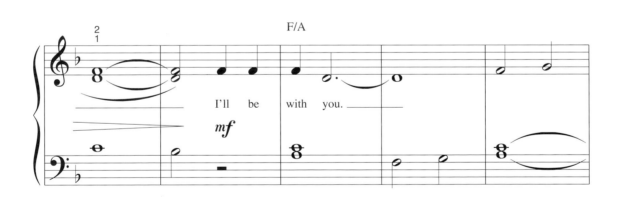

F/A

I'll be with you. ___

mf

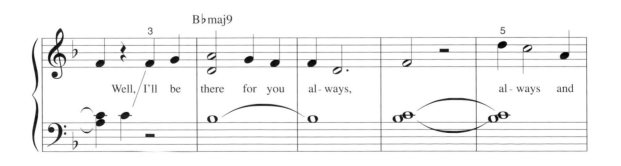

Bbmaj9

Well, I'll be there for you al - ways,　al - ways and

al - ways. _____ Just look o - ver your shoul-

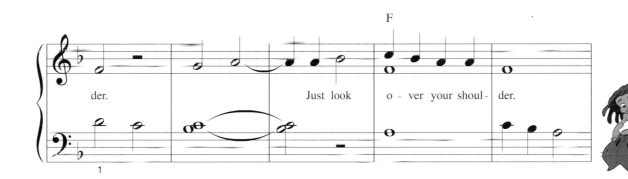

der. Just look o - ver your shoul- der.

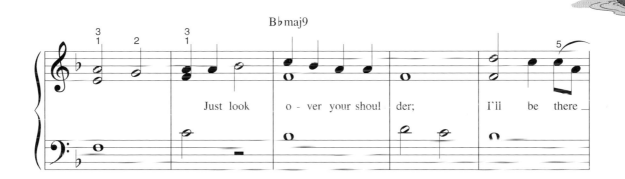

Just look o - ver your shoul der; I`ll be there ___

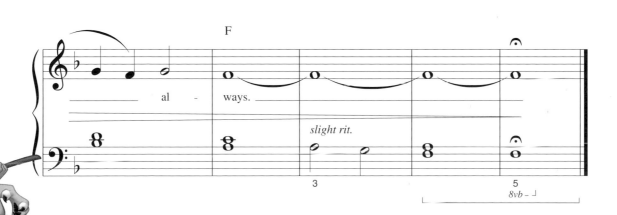

al - ways. _____

slight rit.

WHEN SHE LOVED ME

from Walt Disney Pictures' *Toy Story 2* – A Pixar Film

Music and Lyrics by Randy Newman

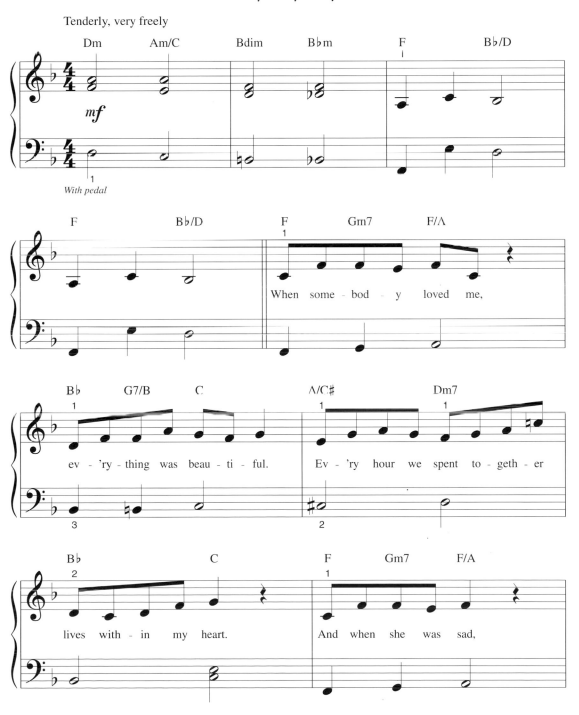

Lyrics under the staff:

When some-bod-y loved me, ev-'ry-thing was beau-ti-ful. Ev-'ry hour we spent to-geth-er lives with-in my heart. And when she was sad,

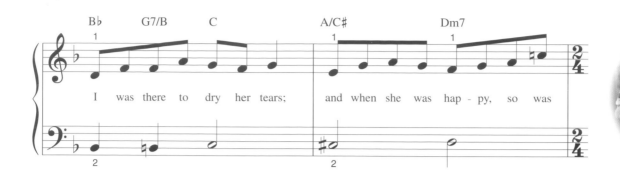

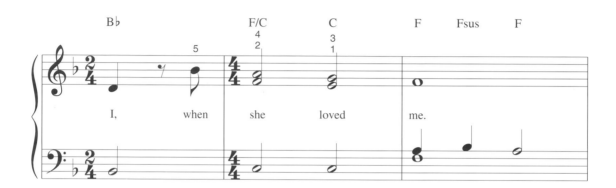

B♭ **F/C** **C** **F** **Fsus** **F**

I, when she loved me.

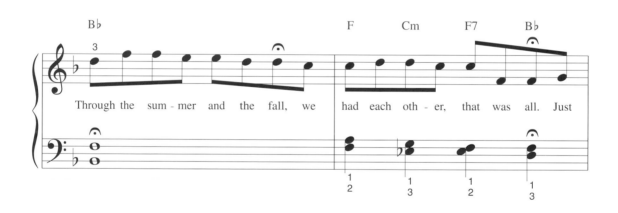

B♭ **F** **Cm** **F7** **B♭**

Through the sum-mer and the fall, we had each oth-er, that was all. Just

F/C **B♭** **F/C** **G7** **C**

she and I to-geth-er, like it was meant to be.

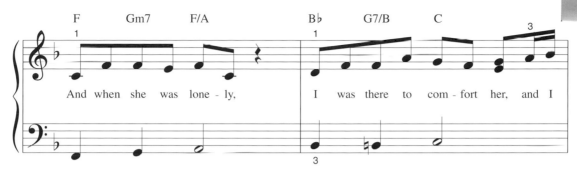

And when she was lone-ly, I was there to com-fort her, and I

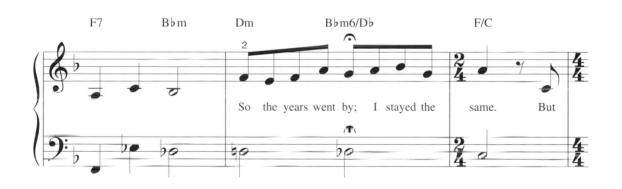

knew that she loved me.

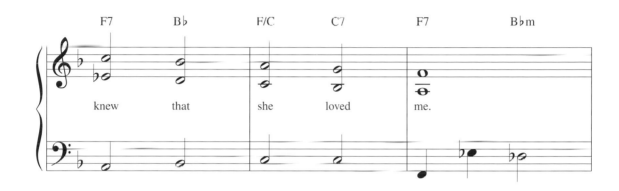

So the years went by; I stayed the same. But

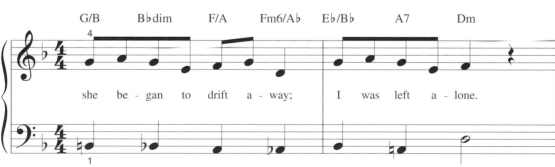

she be-gan to drift a-way; I was left a-lone.

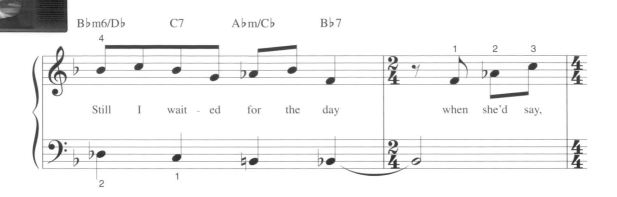

Still I wait - ed for the day when she'd say,

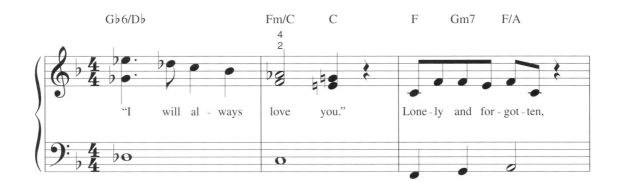

"I will al - ways love you." Lone - ly and for - got - ten,

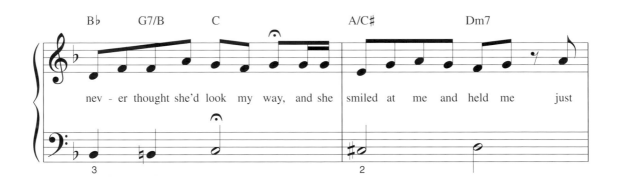

nev - er thought she'd look my way, and she smiled at me and held me just

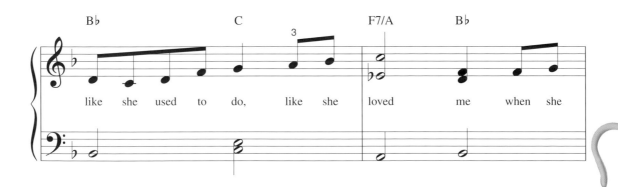

like she used to do, like she loved me when she

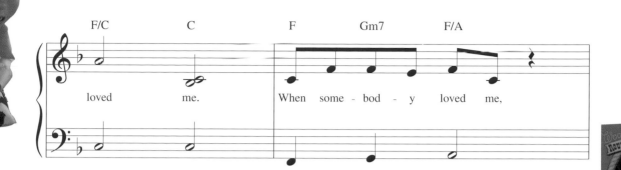

loved me. When some-bod-y loved me,

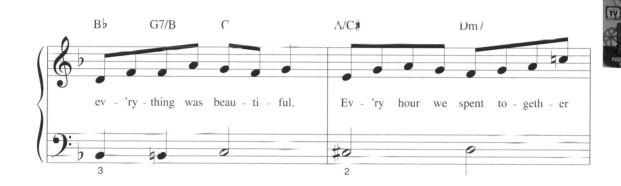

ev-'ry-thing was beau-ti-ful. Ev-'ry hour we spent to-geth-er

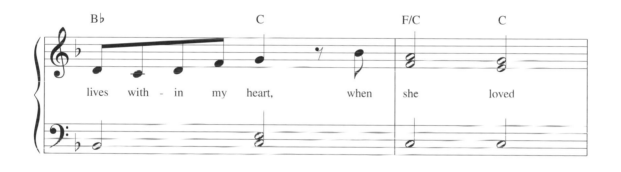

lives with-in my heart, when she loved

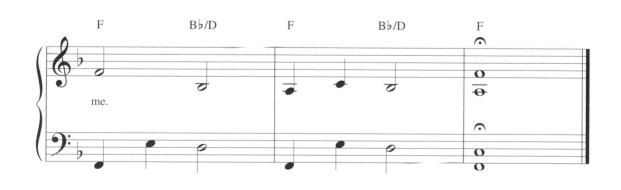

me.

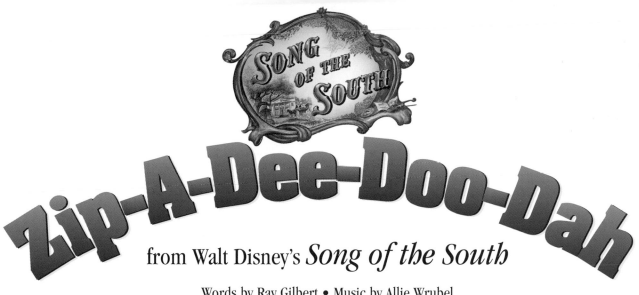

Zip-A-Dee-Doo-Dah

from Walt Disney's *Song of the South*

Words by Ray Gilbert • Music by Allie Wrubel

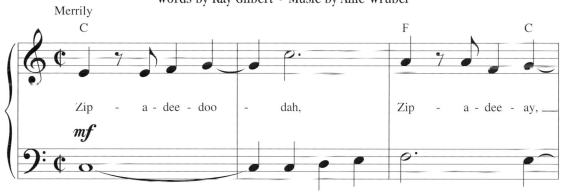

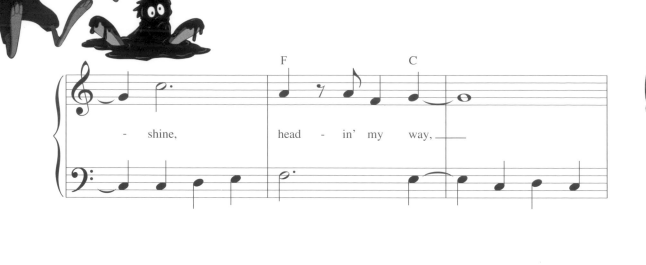
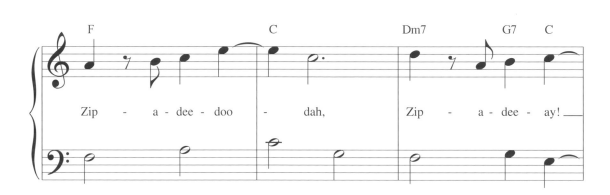
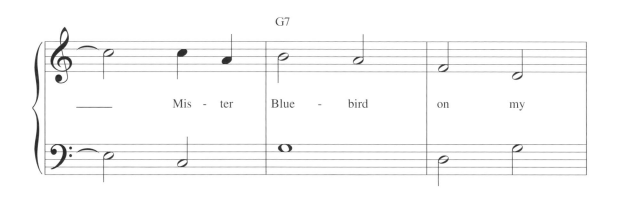

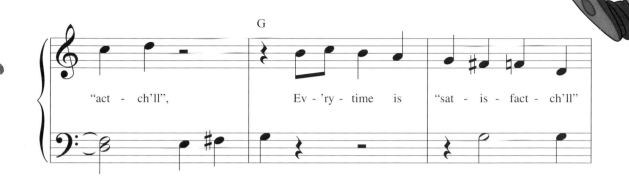

"act – ch'll",   Ev – 'ry – time is   "sat – is – fact – ch'll"

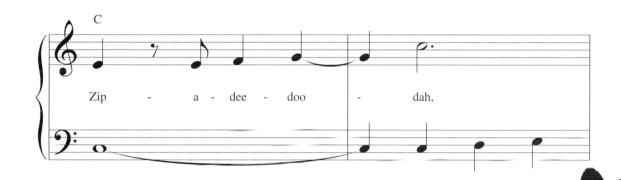

Zip – a – dee – doo – dah,

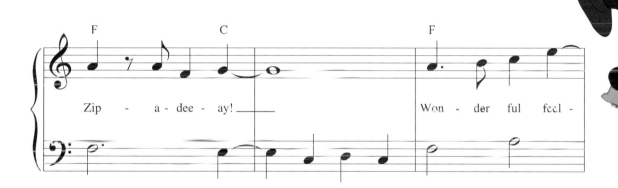

Zip – a – dee – ay!   Won – der – ful feel –

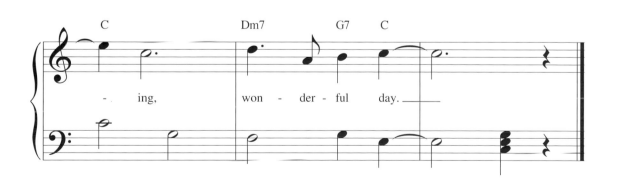

– ing,   won – der – ful day.